WITHDRAWN

Unsolved Political Mysteries

Mysteries and Conspiracies™

UNSOLVED POLITICAL MYSTERIES

David Southwell and Sean Twist

ROSEN PUBLISHING®

New York

North American edition first published in 2008 by:

The Rosen Publishing Group, Inc.
29 East 21st Street
New York, NY 10010

North American edition book design: Tahara Anderson

Library of Congress Cataloging-in-Publication

Southwell, David.
[Conspiracy theories]
Unsolved political mysteries / David Southwell and Sean Twist.—North American ed.
    p.cm.—(Mysteries and conspiracies)
Includes bibliographical references and index.
ISBN-13: 978-1-4042-1083-7
ISBN-10: 1-4042-1083-0
1. United States—Politics and government—1945–1989—Anecdotes—Juvenile literature. 2. United States—Politics and government—1989—Anecdotes—Juvenile literature. 3. Conspiracies–United States—History—20th century—Juvenile literature. 4. Curiosities and wonders—United States—History—20th century–Juvenile literature. 5. United States—History—1945–Anecdotes—Juvenile literature. 6. Politicians—United States-Biography—Anecdotes—Juvenile literature. 7. United States—History—1945—Biography—Anecdotes–Juvenile literature.
I. Twist, Sean. II. Title.
E743.S685 2008
909.82–dc22
                                 2007007850

Manufactured in the United States of America

On the cover: Two unsolved political mysteries include Iraq's Saddam Hussein *(left)* and the invasion of Kuwait and the death of the Organization of Afro-American Unity's leader Malcolm X *(right)*.

CONTENTS

1 MALCOLM X

If you were a controversial political figure in America during the 1960s, it was highly probable that your life would end in a hail of bullets. Malcolm X, the fiery leader of the Organization of Afro-American Unity who outraged white America with his pronouncements on racial matters, was yet another man cut down in his prime because of the dangerous power of his beliefs.

Malcolm X was born Malcolm Little in 1925. His father, a Baptist minister, was murdered by white racists six years later and the family was broken up and put into foster care. Little was a bright student, but his dreams of becoming a lawyer were crushed when a teacher explained to him that he was only a "nigger" and should consider becoming a carpenter instead. Disillusioned with education, he drifted into a life of petty crime. While serving time for burglary, Little began to read about the Nation of Islam (NOI). The

Malcolm X's powerful speeches attracted many to the cause of black power.

NOI's beliefs of black self-reliance and the need for racial separation intrigued Little. When he was released, in 1952, he joined the Nation of Islam, dropping his surname because it was a vestige of slave ownership, and replacing it with a simple "X."

Malcolm X rose quickly through the ranks of the Nation, becoming the organization's chief spokesman. But after his inflammatory comments about John F. Kennedy's assassination, its leader, Elijah Muhammad, suspended him from the NOI. Malcolm X took this opportunity to create his Organization of Afro-American Unity, and did not return to the Nation when his suspension was over.

Where Martin Luther King Jr. believed in nonviolence and the integration of blacks into white America, Malcolm X angered white society by stating that blacks were superior to whites in all ways. He traveled the world, speaking in the Middle East and generating support for a United Nations resolution condemning both South Africa and the United States for human rights violations in their treatment of blacks. Such views, as well as animosity from the Nation of Islam, made Malcolm X a man who was widely hated. This hatred came to a head at a meeting on February 21, 1965, at the Audubon Ballroom in New York.

At the beginning of the meeting, a fight broke out in front of the stage where Malcolm X was speaking. As he tried to calm things down, a group of five assassins stood in the audience and shot him. Malcolm X died shortly afterwards, another figure cut down in America's cull of leaders who threatened the Establishment in the not-so-groovy sixties.

THE STRANGE PART

Even though there was a hospital across the street from the Audubon Ballroom, it still took close to half an hour for an emergency crew to arrive, following X's shooting.

THE USUAL SUSPECTS

The FBI

J. Edgar Hoover, the cross-dressing head of the FBI, distrusted Malcolm X because he represented a force of black power that had no place in Hoover's view of America. One counter-intelligence program sponsored by the FBI was designed to keep a "black messiah" like X from uniting the black movement. With Malcolm X growing closer to Martin Luther King Jr., the FBI could have decided that killing X was the only way to prevent a united black front from arising.

The U.S. Government

The prospect of a U.N. resolution condemning the United States along with South Africa for human rights violations seemed a clear possibility. This would have been embarrassing for the United States. By taking out the chief proponent for this resolution, Malcolm X, the States could then spin-doctor the whole messy business away.

THE UNUSUAL SUSPECTS

The Mob

In an effort to clean up black neighborhoods and institute a lifestyle of clean living, Malcolm X verbally attacked the drug trade. This threat to the profits that could be made from the despair of the ghetto may have sealed X's fate.

The Nation of Islam

The schism between the Nation of Islam and Malcolm X's own group ran deep, with some people feeling that X was unfairly criticizing Elijah Muhammad and other NOI leaders, such as Louis Farrakhan, if not outrightly blaspheming. This could have resulted in a murder that had both political and religious overtones to its motive as some in the Nation of Islam openly fanned this hatred of X.

MOST CONVINCING EVIDENCE

Leon Ameer, a member of the Organization of Afro-American Unity, stated on March 13, 1965, that he had proof of a government connection in Malcolm X's death. Unfortunately,

Ameer's body was found the following morning before he could back up this claim. His death was attributed to an epileptic fit, even though past medical examinations had found no hint of epilepsy.

MOST MYSTERIOUS FACT

Of the three men who were convicted of Malcolm X's murder, one was unable to walk and was at home on the day of the assassination.

SKEPTICALLY SPEAKING

In the United States, if you're black and speak out about human rights, you're a radical. If you're white, you're a humanitarian and get asked to Rotary dinners. No conspiracy is needed to explain this awful truth.

2 Nixon, Watergate, and E. Howard Hunt

Watergate is the most famous political conspiracy of the modern age. The exposure of attempts to cover up a failed conspiracy led to Richard Milhous Nixon becoming the first U.S. president to resign from office. No current political scandal is complete unless it is given the "-gate" tag.

In 1995, when renowned conspiriologist and filmmaker Oliver Stone produced *Nixon*—starring Anthony Hopkins as the unfortunate president—he was not the first theorist to speculate that Watergate was only the visible surface of a much larger and more sinister plot. Like Stone's other conspiracy-fueled opus, *JFK*, the film was condemned by those it portrayed and by the Establishment—a sign taken by Stone's fellow conspiriologists to suggest that it may have contained a great deal of truth.

The facts regarding the outer layer of Watergate are well established and form the basis of the official version of the scandal that is taught even in schools—one of the few conspiracies that the education system acknowledges. In the early hours of June 17, 1972, James McCord—a man with links to the CIA—led a group of four anti-Castro Cuban exiles in an attempt to burgle the Democratic National Committee Headquarters. The burglars were discovered and arrested as they attempted to tap the telephone system in the Watergate office and hotel complex in Washington, D.C.

Charges also were laid against two more people: G. Gordon Liddy, finance counsel to the president and the power behind Nixon's Committee to Re-elect the President (CREEP); and E. Howard Hunt, a former White House aide and ex-CIA operative. Over the next few months, what initially appeared to be a third-rate burglary quickly escalated into a full-blown political scandal. Nixon's involvement in the conspiracy to cover up a conspiracy led to America's gravest constitutional crisis and climaxed with his resignation as president on August 9, 1974.

However, in the national aftermath of distrust following Watergate, conspiracy theorists began to examine the details of the case. They discovered an assortment of facts that suggested the real reason behind the downfall of Nixon was a conspiracy to hide the truth about the assassination of President John F. Kennedy.

THE STRANGE PART

On the Watergate tapes that provided the damning evidence of his involvement in the cover-up of the original burglary, President Nixon says: "Look, the problem is that this [Watergate] will open up the whole Bay of Pigs thing again." John Ehrlichman, assistant to the president for domestic affairs, who served eighteen months in prison for his part in the conspiracy, has admitted that "Bay of Pigs" was Nixon's code phrase for the John F. Kennedy assassination.

Dorothy Hunt, the wife of one of the key players in Watergate, E. Howard Hunt, may have been blackmailing the White House and have demanded more than $1 million to keep silent about information that would "blow the White House out of the water." Many conspiriologists believe that there is photographic evidence to suggest that Hunt, a long-time CIA agent, was one of the famous "Three Tramps" photographed on the grassy knoll immediately after the shooting of JFK.

THE USUAL SUSPECTS

James Jesus Angleton

Director of CIA counterintelligence from 1954 to 1974, James Jesus Angleton is suspected by many of being the mastermind

The Watergate scandal cost Nixon his presidency, but was there much more to it than the public knew?

behind JFK's assassination. His uncharacteristic refusal to help Nixon cover up the White House involvement in the burglary definitely helped seal Nixon's fate. Was Angleton willing to sacrifice a president to hide his involvement in the "whole Bay of Pigs thing"?

The Mafia

It is well established that the Mafia and their Cuban allies had strong links to the CIA and probably played a part in the death of John F. Kennedy, so it is probably more than coincidence that four anti-Castro Cuban exiles were among the Watergate burglars. If the role of high-placed mobsters in the JFK conspiracy were in danger of being exposed by Watergate, they would have a solid motive for wanting Nixon to take all of the blame.

THE UNUSUAL SUSPECTS

Federal Reserve Bank

Lee Harvey Oswald's widow has pointed the finger at the U.S. Federal Reserve Bank's mysterious role in the JFK affair. A private corporation that controls the creation of all American money, the Federal Reserve Bank (FRB) is owned in part by the Rockefellers. Given that the hugely influential Trilateral Commission was set up by David Rockefeller in 1973, some have conjectured that the FRB had the financial and political muscle to stage Watergate to depose Nixon—a possible obstacle in its plans for world domination.

Howard Hughes

In 1972, eccentric millionaire Howard Hughes asked the White House to send the team that eventually bungled the Watergate burglary to break into the office of a Las Vegas newspaper editor, Hank Greenspun. Their task would have been to steal certain papers that formed allegedly devastating blackmail material. Given that some have linked Hughes and his fellow oil barons with Nixon and a plot to kill JFK, his role in Watergate is suspicious to say the least.

MOST CONVINCING EVIDENCE

In December 1973, a United Airlines flight crashed near Chicago Midway Airport. On board was E. Howard Hunt's wife, Dorothy. One of Hunt's fellow Watergate conspirators, Charles Coulson, made a statement to *Time* magazine claiming that "the CIA killed Dorothy Hunt." Unfortunately, his claim may not have been pure paranoia—the pilot of the flight was found to have a quantity of cyanide in his blood that could have been there only if he had been poisoned. Another odd element to the crash is that Dorothy Hunt was carrying more than $250,000 in "hush money" when she boarded the plane, but only $10,000 was recovered with her body.

MOST MYSTERIOUS FACT

A mysterious letter written by Lee Harvey Oswald on November 10, 1963, has been the source of much heated debate. In this note Oswald asks a "Mr. Hunt" for a job within his organization. More than one researcher has come to the conclusion that the letter supplies additional evidence for Hunt's role in the JFK affair.

SKEPTICALLY SPEAKING

Watergate traumatized the American psyche and its scars run deep. The events, which started with that "third-rate burglary," have been described as the root cause in America of the current distrust of government, as well as the tendency to believe in conspiracies. Hardly surprising, then, that Watergate set off further speculation into the JFK assassination.

3 PEARL HARBOR

There are crossroads in time—nexus points—when the actions that take place have the potential to shape the course of history on a grand scale. The events that took place before dawn on Sunday, December 7, 1941, at Pearl Harbor form such a nexus point. They influenced not only the course of World War II, but also the way world history unfolded.

The infamous "sneak attack" by Japanese forces on Hawaii resulted in 2,403 American deaths and 1,178 wounded servicemen; eighteen ships, including three battleships, were sunk; and 188 airplanes were destroyed with a further 162 suffering severe damage. By contrast, the Japanese lost only twenty-nine planes, five midget submarines, and sixty-four men. The direct result of this allegedly surprise attack was a U.S. declaration of war on Japan, which immediately led to

Hitler supporting his Asian allies—an act that finally brought America into the war against the Nazis.

However, some of America's most respected historians have joined forces with the conspiriologists they usually refer to as "delusional paranoids." Both groups suggest that the real reason why Pearl Harbor should be remembered is because it was the tragic outcome of a massive conspiracy to ensure that the United States joined Britain as a full combatant in World War II.

By 1941, the U.S. president, Franklin D. Roosevelt, was faced with a massive and seemingly insurmountable political problem. He wanted America to become involved in the war with Germany, but U.S. public opinion was unsympathetic— Americans felt it was a European affair and that Britain, Russia, and Germany should be left alone to sort it out without any American lives being put at risk. Conspiracy theorists, and some historians, feel that Roosevelt knew Pearl Harbor was going to be attacked, but allowed it to happen as it would give him the perfect excuse for declaring war on Japan—an action that his intelligence services had told him would provoke an identical response from Germany on the United States.

A day that lives in infamy, even in the twenty-first century. The sneak attack by the Japanese is a nexus point that changed the course of world history.

THE STRANGE PART

In 1941, Roosevelt had been warned by his admirals that cutting off the supply of gasoline to Japan was likely to involve the United States in a Pacific war. In July, Roosevelt cut off those petroleum supplies and began to withhold intelligence information about Japanese activities from army and navy officials based in Hawaii. The governments of Britain, Holland, Australia, Peru, Korea, and the Soviet Union all warned the United States that a surprise attack on Pearl Harbor was coming, so it is even more odd that this information was not passed on to the military in Pearl Harbor.

THE USUAL SUSPECTS

Franklin D. Roosevelt

The most obvious suspect in the conspiracy is the president himself. It is no secret that he wanted to bring America into the war with Europe but was being held back by domestic political concerns. His position meant that he had the power to maneuver events in such a way that the United States would not have to fire the first shot and be seen as the aggressor.

Anglo-American Cabal

There is a widespread belief, at least in certain sections of the conspiracy field, that there is a powerful Anglo-American cabal in operation determined to keep the "special relationship" in existence. Believed to involve members of the American and British intelligence services, as well as major figures from business and finance and top politicians, the cabal also may have counted Roosevelt as a member. He could have been instructed to cover up the impending attack on Pearl Harbor so that the United States could be brought into the war to defend Britain.

THE UNUSUAL SUSPECTS

The American Banking Community

At the time of Pearl Harbor, Britain was in debt to America under the terms of the lend-lease agreement. If Britain were defeated by Germany, there would be no chance of it ever repaying the vast loans it had taken out. Therefore, members of the American banking community had a vested interest in British victory and may have pulled strings behind the scenes to ensure America lent more than financial support to their client.

International League of Communists

American conspiracy theorists with a very heavy right-wing bias have believed for some while that Roosevelt was secretly a communist. Their conjecture also makes him a vital member of an alleged International League of Communists, which conspired to take the United States into a war with Germany. America's entry to the war would not be to save democracy in Britain and Europe, but to ensure that the world's first communist state, the Soviet Union, was not crushed by the might of the Nazi war machine.

MOST CONVINCING EVIDENCE

In 1932, a joint U.S. Army-Navy exercise saw Pearl Harbor being successfully "attacked" by 152 planes half an hour before dawn on a Sunday—catching the defenders completely by surprise. This was duplicated in 1938, so there can be no doubt that the military knew the potential risk to Pearl Harbor. Furthermore, the United States had cracked the top Japanese naval and diplomatic codes—a fact not lost on a top-secret Army Board. In 1944, the board reported: "Numerous pieces of information came to our State, War, and Navy Departments in all of their top ranks indicating precisely the intentions of the Japanese, including the probable exact hour and date of the attack."

MOST MYSTERIOUS FACT

The U.S. Navy in Pearl Harbor was laughably underprepared for the attack. Ships were tied up side-by-side and, despite radar operators in Hawaii reporting that Japanese planes were coming, no one took any action. Three American battleships were sunk in the attack, but by 1941, battleships were obsolete and the aircraft carrier was the pinnacle of naval power. It may be significant that no American aircraft carriers were based at Pearl Harbor during the attack—the majority of them were 3,000 miles away, safely stationed at San Diego, which is where a lot of American navy people had wanted the Pearl Harbor ships to be located.

SKEPTICALLY SPEAKING

It is hard to be skeptical over many aspects of the Pearl Harbor conspiracy, but it is also hazardous ever to underestimate the levels of incompetence that can be achieved by the U.S. military and its commander-in-chief: the president.

4 RUDOLF HESS

There are many strange stories surrounding World War II, but few are stranger than that of Rudolf Hess. In many places, the story of Hess reads more like a lost *Monty Python* sketch than the historical details of the activities of a high-ranking member of Hitler's Nazi Party.

Born in Alexandria, Egypt, on April 26, 1894, Hess fell under the spell that Adolf Hitler was weaving over Germany when he first saw him speak in Munich. Hess joined the Nazi Party in 1920, becoming close to Hitler, whom he idolized. This idolatry led Hess to join Hitler in the Beer Hall Putsch of 1923, when Hitler attempted to take over the reins of power of Germany. Instead, they ended up in Landsberg prison.

Hess acted as Hitler's secretary in prison, taking slavish dictation as Hitler composed *Mein Kampf*. Released from prison in 1925, Hess followed Hitler as he built his Nazi power base, continuing to act as his secretary. As Hitler finally attained the power he so desperately craved, in 1932, he appointed Hess chairman of the Central Political Commission of the Nazi Party. Hess also was made a general in the SS for good measure. As Hess continued to follow Hitler with the blind devotion of a puppy, he was rewarded with the position of deputy Führer in 1933.

Hess was determined to do what he perceived best for his beloved Führer: he would negotiate peace with England, by himself, without telling anyone. Borrowing a Messerschmitt ME-110, Hess flew across the North Sea on May 10, 1941. He was headed for Scotland, to meet with the Duke of Hamilton, a casual acquaintance he had met at the Berlin Olympics in 1936. Hess parachuted into Scotland, met a bewildered farmer, and told him he had an important message for the duke.

His peace plan was considered ludicrous by Winston Churchill: that if England let Germany have Europe, then England would be left alone. Disowned by the Nazi Party, and considered half mad by the British authorities, a disheartened Hess was thrown into prison. He was transferred to Germany for the Nuremberg Trials in 1945, where his mental instability was readily apparent. He was sentenced to life in Spandau prison, and reportedly committed

Rudolf Hess was Hitler's right-hand man, so just why did Hess fly to Britain in 1941?

suicide by hanging himself in 1987 at the age of ninety-two. Or did he?

Theories have sprung up that the man who died in 1987 was not Hess, but a body double. Questions also have arisen as to why a man so obviously incompetent was considered such a threat to British authorities.

THE STRANGE PART

Dr. Hugh Thomas, who cared for Hess in Spandau, stated repeatedly that his patient was not Hess, citing the absence of the scars that Hess should have had.

THE USUAL SUSPECTS

House of Windsor

New research undertaken by Lynn Picknett, Clive Prince, and others showed that there was substantial evidence that the king's brother, the Duke of Kent, was actively involved in Hess's peace mission. They also proved that in 1941, the British peace party included most of the royal family. This has given a shot in the arm for conspiracy theorists who think that the House of Windsor was deeply implicated in the Hess affair and that Winston Churchill arranged the death of the Duke of Kent in 1942.

THE UNUSUAL SUSPECTS

Vril Society

This theory states Hess was kept imprisoned by the Germans because he held vital information about secret

Nazi Antarctic bases operated by the occult Vril Society, which included many top Nazis among its members. Although this sounds bizarre, it should be remembered that James Bond creator and member of MI6 Ian Fleming recommended that master occultist Aleister Crowley should lead the interrogation of Hess.

MOST CONVINCING EVIDENCE

Karel Hille, a Dutch journalist, claimed to have files that had been stolen from M16 by none other than Sir Maurice Oldfield himself, ex-head of M16. The files proved that the man who died in Spandau was not Hess but a body double.

MOST MYSTERIOUS FACT

While imprisoned in Britain, Rudolf Hess kept complaining that he felt his food was being poisoned. This was just chalked up to Hess's instability, but if he were being drugged, his food would be the least conspicuous form of administering poison.

SKEPTICALLY SPEAKING

The world actually managed to jail a high-ranking member of Hitler's Nazi Party? No wonder some people don't believe it—they think that other Nazis went to work for the CIA.

5 SADDAM HUSSEIN

On the face of it, the first Gulf War in 1991 was a straightforward conflict. Traditional analysis stems from the view that Saddam Hussein was a classic megalomaniac dictator, who tested the will of the world to halt his expansionist policies by invading Kuwait in August 1990. In response, a global coalition, led by the United States and United Kingdom, united against him. George Bush Sr. referred to this coalition as a "New World Order." During the Gulf War, the United States organized enough military and political power to successfully defeat Hussein and free Kuwait. Yet all is not what it seems when the conspiracy researchers turn their questioning gaze to the Gulf War, up until the second Gulf War in 2003, the largest military campaign undertaken since World War II. A number of significant puzzles develop when certain questions are

asked. For instance, why did Allied forces stop when they could have easily driven into Baghdad? If Hussein was another Hitler, why wait more than a decade to bring about the "regime change" that Bush Jr. was determined to bring about? Accusations and rumors that began when the conspiracy world started to question the established view now have been brought out into the open as accepted, mainstream facts. Even before the tanks hit the Baghdad highway for a second time in 2003, more than one revisionist heavyweight commentator on international politics had begun to wonder if the first Gulf War was set up and carried out for objectives other than freeing Kuwait.

THE STRANGE PART

It generally has become accepted that the U.S. Department of State gave a "green light" to Hussein to invade Kuwait. This happened when an Iraqi ambassador raised the subject of how the United States would react to a potential Iraqi invasion with American ambassador April Glaspie in August 1990, just before Iraqi tanks rolled across the sand.

While debate rages as to the exact details of what occurred at that meeting, whether by intent or accident, it seems certain that Hussein thought that the United States would not object if he went ahead with his invasion plans.

The American government may have let Hussein invade Kuwait.

Given that a number of U.S. senators recently had visited Baghdad and declared support for Hussein—including at least one staunch Jewish liberal and champion of Israel—it is a conclusion he could be forgiven for making.

THE USUAL SUSPECTS

New World Order

The "new world order" was an expression first used in the 1920s by Colonel Edward House, who believed in world government. President George H. W. Bush brought the phrase into the public spotlight when he described the coalition gathered against Saddam as a sign of an emerging New World Order (NWO). Most conspiriologists view the NWO as a form of One World government that secret forces are working to introduce. For a New World Order to hold power over nation states, it would need to be able to justify its existence. The type of international operation of joint political and military force seen in the Gulf may be the first example designed to convince the population of the globe that the NWO is an idea whose time has come.

Military-Industrial Complex

With the fragmentation of the Soviet Union in 1989, and the specter of a communist menace a thing of the past, people were beginning to question whether the United States and its

Western allies actually needed to keep spending billions on defense. Conspiracy theorists believe that the invasion by Saddam Hussein, in 1990, is just too much of a coincidence. They believe that he was put up to the attack on Kuwait by the military-industrial complex, so that he could be presented as the new enemy that needed opposing—hence justifying continued massive spending on armaments.

THE UNUSUAL SUSPECTS

KGB

It is well known that the Soviets and the KGB had developed a very close relationship with Hussein over the years. Some conspiracy theorists believe that the demise of the Soviet Union is merely a diversionary tactic to allow the KGB to develop plans for communist world domination—it was the KGB that arranged the Gulf War. By setting up Hussein as the main bogeyman, the KGB's strategists ensured that American attention would be focused on Iraq, leaving them free to pursue their machinations unmolested by the United States.

Oil Companies

If nothing else, the first Gulf War managed to push the price of crude oil up to the type of figure that the oil companies had not enjoyed since the days of the 1973 oil crisis.

George Bush Sr. made his fortune as oil baron and, with petrochemical industry–intelligence community connections, some have speculated that financial gain may have been the true motive behind the staging of the first Gulf War. With George W. following in his father's footsteps and with his own oil-based fortune, it is not surprising that this is still a popular theory to explain the second Gulf War, too.

MOST CONVINCING EVIDENCE

It is odd that a U.N.-backed coalition of powerful nations could not remove the dictator of one Middle Eastern state, even after smashing his army within a matter of days, especially given that America and Britain were able to topple him later without that powerful backing. It is also strange that in the years subsequent to the first Gulf War, no covert assassination attempt was made on Saddam. Nor was any meaningful military action taken against him or his alleged stocks of chemical and biological weapons until another member of the Bush clan was in the White House. Even at the end of the war, with Baghdad under U.S. control, Saddam was still not in the custody of the United Nations for war crimes against the Kurds.

Finally toppled — but why did the United States leave Hussein in power after the first Gulf War?

MOST MYSTERIOUS FACT

In the aftermath of the Gulf War, an intriguing book entitled *American Hero* was written by Larry Beinhart and published by Ballantine Books. Purporting to be fiction, it details how the war was the idea of a Republican dirty-tricks expert designed to boost the popularity of George Bush Sr. For a novel, its unearthed facts and extensive footnotes provide a damning level of evidence for the conspiracy view of the Gulf War. One question it raises is why did the American, British, and Soviet ambassadors all leave Kuwait two days before the invasion?

SKEPTICALLY SPEAKING

As the second Gulf War showed, America did not come up with good excuses for its invasion of Iraq, so allowing the attack on Kuwait seems a little unnecessary. Maybe the reason why Hussein was left in power at the end of the first Gulf War was because George Bush Sr. wanted to leave his son something to get his teeth into when he became president?

6 HILLARY CLINTON

When Hillary Rodham Clinton announced during a major televised interview that she and her husband, Bill Clinton, were "victims of a vast right-wing conspiracy," she became the most famous supporter of a conspiracy theory in the world. But if she thought her shattering accusation, which stunned the American media, might gain her some sympathy and support from the hordes of conspiriologists who took an interest in her career, she was very mistaken.

Hillary's favored conspiracy theory saw her and her husband being attacked by a dark network of right-wingers. The conspiracy took in everyone from the editors of British tabloids to television evangelist Jerry Falwell. In her mind, the media interest in the Monica Lewinsky and Paula Jones sexual harassment charges against Bill Clinton and the long-running

Next stop . . . the White House? Where will Hillary Clinton's political ambitions take her?

investigation by independent counsel Kenneth Starr into the Whitewater scandal were "politically motivated."

G. Gordon Liddy, one of the key players in the Watergate conspiracy, used his radio show to disclose that he used pictures of the First Lady for target practice and called her a "broomstick-riding witch." Most conspiracy theorists, however, disagreed that this was proof of evil forces working against her. They were much more interested in digging out details surrounding a large number of people who had known or worked with her and had subsequently died under suspicious circumstances.

Compiling what became known in conspiracy circles as the "Clinton Body Count," researchers were startled to find that being a friend of Bill or Hillary Clinton seemed to be one of the most dangerous occupations on the planet. This was definitely the case if you had been involved in the Whitewater investment scandal or possessed evidence about the state of their marriage or love lives.

When President Clinton and his wife finally were cleared of acting illegally in the Arkansas land deal that became known as Whitewater, it was in large part due to the fact that many of the key witnesses were dead. The Whitewater land deal was a failed Arkansas property venture in which the Clintons were involved when he was governor of the state in the 1980s and Mrs. Clinton was a partner in a local law firm. After the highly convenient deaths, the evidence that remained "was insufficient to prove to a jury beyond a reasonable doubt that either the President or Mrs. Clinton knowingly participated in any criminal conduct." However, according to the final report, "troubling questions remained over aspects of the deal" and "the Clintons should have known that something was wrong with their investments and made statements that were factually inaccurate." It was highly fortunate for Hillary that no charges were brought against her as it would have almost stopped her from becoming a senator for New York and using the position as a stepping stone to her campaign to run for president. However, as Hillary continues to make political progress, the doubts produced by the "Clinton Body Count" refuse to go away. Could someone be silencing those who could embarrass her and prove an obstacle to America's First Lady making history as the first female occupant of the Oval Office?

THE STRANGE PART

Alongside two of the most notorious suicides in the annals of conspiracy research (those of investigative reporter Danny Casolaro and Vince Foster, former White House counsel, and colleague of Hillary Clinton at her Little Rock law firm), the shooting of Mary Caitrin Mahoney may have spared Hillary some further blushes. Mahoney was a former White House intern and her death came just days after it was rumored that she was planning to disclose the story behind her sexual harassment. She was killed, along with two Starbucks employees, in a Washington branch of the coffee chain in a reputed robbery where nothing was taken. Mahoney was shot five times; one of the shots was to the back of her head, gangland execution style. FBI agent Bradley Garrett arrested Carl Derek Cooper for the three murders, and after fifty-four hours of questioning by Garrett and another agent, Cooper signed a confession that he immediately repudiated as soon as he got to court. Garrett was later put in charge of the Chandra Levy case.

THE USUAL SUSPECTS

Fourth International

As a student, Hillary supported a raft of extreme causes, including the Black Panthers, and attended events organized by admirers of communism. Some suspect that the former radical firebrand was recruited to join the secretive communist cadre the Fourth International. Allegedly created by Trotsky to bring about through stealth a global communist state, Hillary could be the Fourth International's most likely chance of putting a secret communist in the Oval Office and starting the United States on an incremental path toward socialism.

THE UNUSUAL SUSPECTS

Feminist Lesbian Sisterhood

Hillary is a secret lesbian, her marriage to Bill a sham arranged for their mutual political convenience, Chelsea Clinton a hired child actor, and the ultimate aim of Hillary is nothing less than to become the first female president of the USA. According to this line of conspiratorial thought, Hillary is the front woman for a fascist feminist lesbian group known as "The Sisterhood," which also includes Cherie Blair. Once Hillary is in the White House, The Sisterhood will use the massive powers of the president to instigate a coup and begin a matriarchal dictatorship.

The Medical Establishment

During her husband's two terms as president, Hillary Clinton took control of U.S. health policy and tried to instigate radical changes in the health-care system, even though she was not elected to any office. Seeing freedom to choose their own doctors and medical insurance providers taken out of their hands, some were convinced that Hillary was working on behalf of the medical establishment to further consolidate its control and enhance its power of life and death. With Hillary's support from medical experimentation and cloning, they fear new medical horrors would be guaranteed if she ever made it to the highest position in the land.

MOST CONVINCING EVIDENCE

Former Democratic National Committee fund-raiser Ron Brown was a close associate of Hillary. When he came under criminal investigation and indictment seemed imminent, Brown reportedly told a confidante that he would "take her down with me." Days later, his plane crashed on the approach to Dubrovnik airport during a trade mission excursion to

Croatia. Unable to draw firm conclusions, some military forensic investigators were alarmed by what appeared to be a .45-caliber bullet hole in the top of Brown's head.

MOST MYSTERIOUS FACT

A poll conducted among thousands of Americans to find out who they thought was the most evil person of the millennium produced some interesting results. Not surprisingly, Hitler came in first, but Hillary appeared in sixth position, way ahead of Saddam Hussein, Charles Manson, the Marquis de Sade, and Idi Amin.

SKEPTICALLY SPEAKING

Self-claimed victim of a vast conspiracy or perpetrator of one to kill anyone who could harm her chances of claiming the presidency? Even if Hillary left politics behind and joined a nunnery, there's a strong chance that nothing would change— she would still be the second-most name-dropped woman in the conspiracy field, just behind Queen Elizabeth II.

7 GEORGE BUSH SR.

Anyone elected to the office of president of the United States of America becomes the center of attention for an army of conspiriologists. George Bush Sr. was something of an exception—even before he was elected as Ronald Reagan's vice president in 1980, he was already at the heart of several major conspiracy theories including Watergate, the Bay of Pigs, and the assassination of JFK.

Officially, Bush only worked for the Central Intelligence Agency from 1976–77 when he was its director. However, there is a large body of evidence to suggest that he was working for the CIA as early as 1961. He was a member of the bizarre Skull and Bones Society at college—a known recruiting ground for senior CIA agents. Running his oil company meant visiting rigs across the world—the perfect cover for an agent. His company was named Zapata, which was also the code name for the CIA's Bay of Pigs operation. The two Navy ships repainted as civilian ships for the aborted invasion attempt were renamed *Barbara* and *Houston*—the names of Bush's wife and of the town in Texas where his company was based.

When the U.S. government released nearly 100,000 pages of documents on the Kennedy assassination in 1978, conspiracy researchers found a memo among them from the State Department to "George Bush of the Central Intelligence Agency." This memo warned of the possibility that anti-Castro groups in Miami might stage another invasion of Cuba in the aftermath of the JFK murder. President Bush has denied that he was the man in the memo and that it was intended for another "George Bush" who also had a similar address to him. Conspiracy buffs believe that the memo was sent to the CIA because of the previous invasion attempt and to George Bush because he was involved in the planning of other invasions, including the Bay of Pigs.

Another significant Bush link to the Kennedy affair lies with George de Mohrenschildt, a rich Russian oilman and longtime CIA agent who lived in Texas and helped Lee Harvey Oswald settle there after he left the Soviet Union. Shortly before he was due to testify before the House Select Committee on Assassinations, de Mohrenschildt was found dead of an allegedly self-inflicted gunshot wound. His personal address book contained the entry: "Bush, George H. W. (Poppy) 1412 W. Ohio also Zapata Petroleum Midland."

Given this type of security service background to investigate, it is not surprising that some conspiriologists believe that the then Vice President Bush was the force behind a

conspiracy to assassinate President Ronald Reagan in 1982, in an attempt to place himself in the White House a few years ahead of schedule.

THE STRANGE PART

The official version of events on March 30, 1982, is that Reagan was walking to his limousine when John Hinckley Jr. surged forward and opened fire with a pistol. A bullet allegedly ricocheted off the limousine and injured Reagan, but it failed to kill him. However, more than one witness reported that at least one shot came from a Secret Service agent who was stationed on the overhang behind Reagan's limousine. As one beneficiary of Reagan's death would have been Bush, conspiracy buffs have made him (or forces controlling him) the prime suspect in the Reagan shooting.

THE USUAL SUSPECTS

The CIA

The traditional bad guys of the conspiracy world certainly have played a big part in the life of George Bush Sr. It is possible the agency wished to put one of their men into the White House early to help them strengthen their position in the drug

Before becoming president of the United States of America, George Bush had already served as the director of the CIA.

trade and secret wars they were conducting in Central America at the time of the shooting. The CIA already may have eliminated more than one president—JFK through an assassin's bullet, and Nixon by the Watergate scandal—so would have little reason to doubt it could be done again without comeback.

Skull and Bones

It is well known that George Bush Sr. was a member of the Skull and Bones—a secret society at Yale college with initiation rites that involve lying naked in a coffin and providing fellow members with a list of blackmail material against you. Members of the Skull and Bones have a tendency to form the ruling elite of America, and the society seems to operate as an unofficial recruiting body for the U.S. intelligence community. No one knows exactly what the true aim of the Skull and Bones is, but placing one of its own in the White House does not sound too unlikely a goal.

THE UNUSUAL SUSPECTS

MJ-12

Allegedly the true ruling power in America and the group behind the cover-up of the existence of UFOs and aliens, MJ-12 may have wanted to eliminate Reagan because he was unstable and could have exposed the group's existence. It is certain that Reagan came close to implying the reality of an alien menace when he made a speech suggesting that the USA and USSR would be forced to unite in a moment if the people of the world discovered that they had a common extraterrestrial enemy. MJ-12 is rumored to always include the current director of the CIA on its controlling committee, which, if true, would have made Bush a former member of the organization.

Knights of Malta

An allegedly Catholic organization based around the Knights of the Hospital of St. John of Jerusalem, which was created during the Crusades, membership of the Knights of Malta at the time of Reagan's shooting included head of the CIA, William Casey, and Reagan's foreign policy chief, General Alexander Haig. Confusion reigned in the aftermath of the shooting as to who, exactly, was in control of America while Reagan was disabled. When asked about this, Haig said, "I'm in charge now." Were the Knights of Malta behind the shooting as part of a plot to install a president who was an ex-CIA man with close links to certain "Knights"?

MOST CONVINCING EVIDENCE

If you inspect the video footage of the shooting, it is clear that from the position Hinckley was standing in when he opened fire that he would have needed to shoot through a car door to hit Reagan where he did. This impossibility is

Another U.S. president shot—this time Ronald Reagan—and another alleged lone gunman. No wonder some see a conspiracy.

explained by the "ricochet theory," which is as implausible as the infamous "magic bullet theory" in the JFK shooting.

MOST MYSTERIOUS FACT

Members of the Bush and Hinckley families were very old friends as both families had made their fortunes in the Texas oil boom. The families shared many connections, and it may be more than just a rather spooky coincidence that George

Bush's son Neil was supposed to have had dinner with Scott Hinckley—John Hinckley's brother—the evening that John attempted to shoot President Ronald Reagan.

SKEPTICALLY SPEAKING

Anyone whose hero is Travis Bickle and who is obsessed with Jodie Foster deserves the label "nut" and is probably unbalanced enough to attempt the lone assassination of a president. The fact that George Bush Sr. is connected to the CIA by a large number of supposed links and secret societies just helps to create the illusion of conspiracy where there is no real evidence for one.

8 THE EUROPEAN UNION

The authors of this book never expected to have their words on a conspiracy used in a speech by Margaret Thatcher, the most right-wing prime minister ever elected to office in the United Kingdom. Then again, you should expect surprises when working in the conspiracy field. However, it did not come as a surprise to some conspiracy theorists when, in 2002, the Iron Lady claimed that the European Union (EU) was part of a secret plot—possibly instigated by the Nazis—to take control of the people of Europe and strip them of political rights. After all, it was exactly what they had been saying for years.

The creation of the euro—the single currency for the eurozone—and the planned expansion of the EU, from fifteen to twenty-five countries, persuaded more and more conspiracy theorists to turn their scrutiny on the dream of European political and economic harmony. With Latvia, Malta, Slovenia, Hungary,

Lithuania, Slovakia, Poland, the Czech Republic, Estonia, and Cyprus joining and, therefore, pushing the EU both farther east and farther south, the fear that there may be more to the EU than we have been told has become the concern of many throughout the world.

The official view of the history of the European Union claims that it grew out of an initial plan by France and Germany to pool all their coal and steel production under a joint authority as a sign of cooperation and friendship after World War II. However, even the European Steel and Coal Community of 1950 showed early grand plans. Its founding declaration reads: "The contribution which an organized and living Europe can bring to civilization is indispensable to the maintenance of peaceful relations. Europe will not be made all at once, or according to a single, general plan. It will be built through concrete achievements . . ."

Many thought the direct ancestor of the EU—the European Economic Community—would be a purely economic and technical organization. It was envisioned as covering such issues as common standards for tomato paste or safety in steel plants, so little or no provision was made for the inclusion of a democratic element in the Treaty of Rome, which founded the organization in 1956. However, by the end of the Cold War, the EEC had evolved into the EU, which is now responsible for more than 80 percent of economic and social legislation—and it has a massive impact on the lives of all those who live within its borders.

THE STRANGE PART

There is now little doubt even among Europhiles that the European Union is eroding the importance of the centuries-old nation states that form its membership. It's also clear that the new ruling body is a long way from offering true democratic representation to its millions of citizens. These consequences of the current EU setup uncannily echo the type of aims that many conspiracy theorists claim shadowy organizations like the Illuminati have been struggling to achieve for countless centuries.

THE USUAL SUSPECTS

Priory of Sion

This mysterious, Europe-wide secret society, which has links with everyone in European conspiracy history from the Knights Templar to the Freemasons and the Illuminati, may be the true force behind the rise of the EU. Allegedly the guardian of the bloodline of Christ, the Priory of Sion may exist to establish a United States of Europe ruled over by a monarchical dynasty descended from none other than Jesus Christ. While some of the wilder conspiracy theorists are not entirely certain about

Nazi economics minister and war criminal Walther Funk planned to introduce a system of European economic union after Germany won the war.

the Priory of Sion's role as keeper of a messianic genetic heritage, few of them disagree about the influence and power the priory wields in the murky world of European and international politics.

The Nazis

It is interesting to note that Hitler's ultimate plan after he had defeated his opponents was to establish a "Europe of Regions." The plan for this proposed European Union—the *Europaischewirtschaftgemeinschaft*—was published in book form by the Nazis in 1942. Written primarily by Nazi economics minister and war criminal Walther Funk, the book—entitled *The European Community*—echoed Goering's talk of a post-war project for the "large-scale economic unification of Europe." Goebbels was also fond of saying, "In 50 years Europe will be unified and people will no longer think in terms of countries." With these facts established, it is easy to understand why some conspiracy buffs feel that the EU is a dark plot run by a cabal of deep Nazi agents who infiltrated the governments of Europe at the end of World War II.

Many feel the European Parliament was a sham with no real power hiding a conspiracy based on Nazi plans.

THE UNUSUAL SUSPECTS

The Vatican

The idea of a united Europe is not exactly a modern idea—
it has existed in the past in the form of the Holy Roman
Empire, as a confederation of European states where the
real power lay with the Roman Catholic Church. More than
one conspiracy buff with an antipapal bent has seen the
hand of the Vatican at work within the EU and theorized
that the Church is trying to recreate its glory days by restoring
the Holy Roman Empire under a new name. Of course,
evidence of this conspiracy is hard to find, but then again
most established religions have a good record of covering
their tracks when pulling a fast one.

Aliens from Sirius

Some conspiracy theorists who have read the works of the
mysterious Gerard de Sede believe that the EU is creating
a United States of Europe so that the ancient Merovingian
dynasty can sweep back into power in the twenty-first century.
While the Priory of Sion believes the dynasty is linked to the
family of Jesus Christ, followers of de Sede feel that the
Merovingians are the descendants of extraterrestrials from
Sirius. So, it is those aliens that are pulling the strings to get
their distant family members back into the business of ruling
lesser mortals.

MOST CONVINCING EVIDENCE

More than four decades after it was founded, the EU is less popular now than it has ever been. Fewer than half the voters in Europe think that their country's membership in the EU is a good thing, or that their country benefits from EU membership. While the majority of citizens disagree with the concept, they also think that European integration is inevitable. They also feel that a European policy elite brought about the institution behind closed doors in chancelleries and conference centers. Given that very few direct votes have been taken on the subject of the EU, its growth does seem more like the work of a conspiracy than the exercise of the European people's democratic will.

MOST MYSTERIOUS FACT

In 1973, Swiss journalist Matthiew Paoli began investigating the links between the EEC, one of its bureaucratic entities—the Committee to Protect the Rights and Privileges of Low-Cost Housing—the Grand Lodge Alpina of Freemasonry, and General de Gaulle (one of the prime movers behind the EEC). He published the results of his investigation as the book *Les Dessous*—undercurrents—and left Europe in fear of his safety. On assignment in Israel, he was arrested by Mossad, found guilty of spying without trial, and shot.

SKEPTICALLY SPEAKING

If bureaucracy, centralized power, and undemocratic decision-making constitute a conspiracy, then all governments—and not just the European Union—deserve to be branded as conspiracies. Under these circumstances, it seems unfair for the conspiracy buffs to make the EU seem any worse than the rest.

9 GEORGE W. BUSH

George W. Bush might not have been born to be president as some claim, but the moment he decided to run for the job, he was destined to play a huge role in the theories of many conspiriologists. Even mainstream media, with articles entitled "Born to Be King" and concerned editorials, continue to raise the fact that if the next president after Bush is Hillary Clinton, just two families will have run America for the last twenty years or more. A large section of the public, as well as hardened conspiracy buffs, sense that there was more to the election of the son of former President George Bush Sr. than the quirky workings of democracy. Suspicions about how he came to follow in his father's footsteps are only intensified by the frankly dubious way in which he triumphed in the presidential election against Al Gore and the strange sense that fighting a war in Iraq seems to be a bit of a Bush family tradition.

Bush Jr. has a conspiracy pedigree second to none. Before he even became president, his father was suspected of being involved in the assassination of JFK, Watergate, the Iran-Contra scandal, and the attempted assassination of Ronald Reagan, and he announced the creation of a "New World Order" on the White House lawn. His grandfather—Prescott Bush—made a fortune from Nazi money-laundering activities while Bush Jr. profited from his oil companies' links to Osama bin Laden's brother in Saudi Arabia.

Within minutes of announcing his candidacy for president, conspiracy theorists were speculating online that the coming election would be fixed for a Bush win, a new war on Iraq would be started, and the government would gain further powers—all predictions that seemed to have been accurately fulfilled. The only thing they disagreed about was who was pulling the strings behind the scenes. The assumption was that a man famous for making statements such as, "I know the human being and fish can coexist peacefully," and "It's clearly a budget—it's got a lot of numbers in it," was not the brains behind any plot to gain control of the White House.

The first prediction of a conspiracy to fix the vote exploded in a very public way when the Democratic contender for president, Al Gore, won the national vote by more than a half million votes. However, Bush was installed in the White House due to the result in Florida—a Republican-controlled

Like father like son? A case of spot the difference as Bush Jr. emulated father and took America into war against Iraq.

state where his brother, Jeb, was governor—that swung the electoral college. Amid lost votes, faulty voting machines that counted a vote for Bush, even when a voter selected another candidate, Bush's chance of becoming president hung in the balance as his lead dwindled to a few hundred votes in Florida. Al Gore began pushing for a recount, so Bush supporters in Miami started to riot. The prospect of spreading violence helped influence the U.S. Supreme Court to a 5–4 ruling on stopping a statewide Florida recount and, therefore, making Bush the president. However, it later emerged that the "Brooks Brothers' Riot"—named after the preppie style of the protesters' clothes—was led by so-called rioters who were paid by Bush's election committee. Thus, the organization spent $1.2 million to fly operatives to Florida and elsewhere, and a fleet of corporate jets was assembled, including planes owned by Enron, then run by Kenneth Lay, a major backer of Bush. One of the rioters, Matt Schlapp, even ended up as special assistant to the president.

Once in the White House, the conspiracy community, mindful of the words of David Rockefeller that "We are on the verge of a global transformation. All we need is the right major crises and the nations will accept a New World Order," speculated that something akin to the aborted Operation Northwoods would soon materialize to allow for a war in Iraq and a clampdown on civil liberties.

Northwoods was a secret military plan. It was sanctioned by the joint chiefs of staff but never given presidential clearance to create a public and international climate for an attack on Cuba by hijacking planes, blowing up a U.S. ship, and even committing terrorist acts in U.S. cities and then blaming them on Fidel Castro.

THE STRANGE PART

After 9/11, it was not long before other elements of the conspiracy theorists' earlier predictions began to take shape. The president—who once said, "There ought to be limits to freedom"—brought in the Homeland Security Act. Among other things, this allows for secret arrest and detention, mandatory vaccinations while giving vaccine manufacturers immunity from prosecution, and for the monitoring of all personal communications and financial transactions—even library records. So, there was no surprise when the war against Iraq materialized on the basis that Saddam Hussein was readying weapons of mass destruction to attack the Western world.

THE USUAL SUSPECTS

The Skull and Bones

Like father like son, George W. Bush is working on behalf of the Yale-based Skull and Bones Secret Society. Aside from performing strange rituals akin to esoteric Freemasonry mixed with occult Nazi ceremonies, and obtaining blackmail

Democracy in action? George W. Bush's election to the White House was decided in the state of Florida, where his brother was governor.

material on all members, its aims remain well hidden. However, with two recent presidents and a host of America's ruling elite coming from within its ranks, its connection to power is obvious.

CIA and American Oil Companies

As the CIA shaped the direction of his father's life and presidency, it is not unreasonable to believe that the CIA and its real paymasters in certain American oil companies are repeating history and pulling the strings for "Dubya." Wars benefiting U.S. oil companies in Afghanistan and Iraq, and more power and money for the CIA have been noticeable outcomes of George II's time in the White House.

THE UNUSUAL SUSPECTS

The British Royal Family

America's position as the most powerful, democratic country ever to have existed in world history is a cleverly constructed illusion. The Bush family is part of a network of bloodlines owing loyalty to the British monarchy, who just pretended to lose the war of American Independence. The president's real job is to advocate policies that ensure the continuing success of the secret British Empire and bolster the finances of the House of Windsor.

Reptilian Aliens

George W. Bush is the latest in a line of puppet rulers installed in positions of power by reptilian aliens from the Draco system, who have been secretly running most of the world since 4000 BCE.

MOST CONVINCING EVIDENCE

Unofficial recounts by news organizations found that if all the legally cast ballots in Florida had been counted, Gore would have won Florida and thus the presidency. American citizens now have less freedom than at any previous time in their history. Despite spending more than $500 million post the second Gulf War on weapon inspection, no evidence that Saddam Hussein had massive stockpiles of weapons of mass destruction and was planning an attack has been produced to back up the official reasons for the war.

MOST MYSTERIOUS FACT

"Boy George," as many conspiracy theorists have taken to calling George W. Bush, was so worried about his past surfacing that he hired a private detective to investigate himself. No details of what the detective found have emerged, apart from the fact that as one person of the Bush campaign team said, "No handcuffs or dwarf orgies were found." However, Bush's private detective might be a little worried as four other independent investigators looking into his past all died in suspicious or unexplained circumstances.

SKEPTICALLY SPEAKING

Did Dr. Evil take over the world? Has everything we have been experiencing for the last few years just been a part of his cunning plan—including Mini-Me sitting in the Oval Office? It makes as much sense as some other George W. theories and at least explains why Dubya seems to have problems speaking English properly.

GLOSSARY

Black Panthers Members of the Black Panther Party, an African American organization that was founded in 1966 to advocate civil rights and self-defense. Members called for a violent revolution as the only means by which African Americans could achieve liberation.

bogeyman A terrifying or dreaded person.

cabal A group of people secretly plotting something or united to bring about some form of intrigue.

conspiriologist A conspiracy theorist who has taken an interest in researching the truth behind various dark plots.

counterintelligence An intelligence service's organized activity designed to block an enemy's sources of information, to deceive the enemy, to prevent sabotage, and to gather political and military information.

esoteric Intended for or understood by only a small group.

Establishment An exclusive group of powerful people who rule a government or society by means of private agreements and decisions; an influential group that tacitly, or silently, controls a given field of activity, usually in a conservative manner.

Freemasons Members of the Free and Accepted Masons, an international secret fraternity.

Führer A leader; especially the title of Adolf Hitler as the leader of the German Nazis.

Illuminati The organization founded in Bavaria in 1776; any underground intellectual movement or secret society. The term often is used to describe any hidden elite aiming for world domination and possessing enlightenment.

Iran-Contra scandal Also called the Iran-Contra Affair, this scandal involved the National Security Council of the United States, which had secret weapon transactions and other activities that were prohibited by U.S. law. A part of the money received from weapon sales was diverted by the NSC and given to the Contras, who were U.S.-supported rebels fighting to overthrow the government of Nicaragua.

Knights Templar Members of an order of knights founded in 1119 to protect pilgrims in the Holy Land during the second Crusade and suppressed in 1312; members of an order of Freemasons claiming descent from these medieval knights.

lend-lease agreement The aid program during World War II through which the United States provided food, munitions, and other goods and services to countries whose defense against Germany and Italy was considered necessary to the United States according to the Lend-Lease Act passed on March 11, 1941.

megalomaniac A person with a delusional mental disorder that is marked by feelings of omnipotence and grandeur.

military-industrial complex (MIC) An informal alliance of the military and related government departments with defense industries that is held to influence government policy.

Mini-Me The cloned villain of the Austin Powers's movies.

MI6 The British security service, also known as the Secret Intelligence Service or Her Majesty's Secret Service, and originally called Military Intelligence [section] 6, which is responsible for collecting foreign intelligence relating to national security.

Monty Python The name of an acclaimed British TV show *Monty Python's Flying Circus,* which was broadcast from 1969 to 1974 and was a mix of verbal and physical comedy sketches with animation. The phenomenon of Monty Python became widely popular and resulted in stage shows, film series, recordings, books, and a musical.

Mossad Hebrew for "Central Institute for Intelligence and Security," the Mossad is one of Israel's five chief intelligence organizations and is concerned with espionage, the gathering of intelligence, and secret political operations in foreign nations.

Priory of Sion An alleged 1,000-year secret society that is featured in numerous conspiracy theories. It was supposedly created in the eleventh century to protect and preserve a secret involving the bloodline of Jesus Christ. The priory was believed to have formed the medieval order of the Knights Templar as its military arm.

pronouncements Authoritative announcements or opinions.

Putsch A secretly plotted and suddenly executed attempt to overthrow a government.

right-wing The rightist division of a group or party; people professing support of the established order and favoring traditional attitudes and practices and conservative governmental policies.

schism A division or separation.

SS The Schutzstaffel, an elite Nazi unit whose members served as Hitler's bodyguards and who were later given authority to take charge of intelligence, central security, police activities, and the mass extermination of those they considered inferior or undesirable.

Travis Bickle A fictional character and protagonist of Martin Scorsese's film *Taxi Driver* (1976).

Vril Society A mystical order said to have had an influence on the formation of the ideology of many important members of the Nazi Party. It is frequently mentioned in connection with secret Nazi flying-saucer technology.

FOR MORE INFORMATION

Cold War International History Project
Woodrow Wilson Center
One Woodrow Wilson Plaza
1300 Pennsylvania Avenue NW
Washington, DC 20004-3027
(202) 691-4110
Web site: http://www.wilsoncenter.org/index.cfm?topic_id=
    1409&fuseaction=topics.home

Federal Bureau of Investigation (FBI)
J. Edgar Hoover Building
935 Pennsylvania Avenue NW
Washington, DC 20535-0001
(202) 324-3000
Web site: http://www.fbi.gov

John F. Kennedy Presidential Library and Museum
Columbia Point
Boston, MA 02125
(866) JFK-1960
Web site: http://www.jfklibrary.org

National Archives and Records Administration
8601 Adelphi Road
College Park, MD 20740-6001
(866) 272-6272
Web site: http://www.archives.gov

WEB SITES

Due to the changing nature of Internet links, Rosen Publishing has developed an online list of Web sites related to the subject of this book. This site is updated regularly. Please use this link to access the list:

http://www.rosenlinks.com/cm/unpm

For Further Reading

Belzer, Richard. *UFOs, JFK, and Elvis: Conspiracies You Don't Have to Be Crazy to Believe.* New York, NY: Ballantine, 2000.

Bondesan, Jan. *The Great Pretenders: The True Stories Behind Famous Historical Mysteries.* New York, NY: W. W. Norton, 2004.

Burnett, Thom, ed. *Conspiracy Encyclopedia: The Encyclopedia of Conspiracy Theories.* New York, NY: Chamberlain Bros., 2005.

Elish, Dan. *The Watergate Scandal* (Cornerstones of Freedom). New York, NY: Scholastic, 2004.

Hidell, Al, and Joan D'Arc. *The Complete Conspiracy Reader: From the Deaths of JFK and John Lennon to Government-Sponsored Alien Cover-Ups.* New York, NY: MJF Books, 2003.

Levy, Joel. *The Little Book of Conspiracies: 50 Reasons to Be Paranoid.* New York, NY: Thunder's Mouth Press, 2005.

McConnachie, James, and Robin Tudge. *The Rough Guide to Conspiracy Theories 1* (Rough Guides). London, England: Rough Guides, 2005.

Tuckett, Kate. *Conspiracy Theories.* New York, NY: Berkley, 2005.

INDEX

H

Hess, Rudolf, suicide of, 26–30
Hitler, Adolf, 26–27, 30, 33, 58
Hunt, E. Howard, 13, 15, 17–18
"hush money," 17
Hussein, Saddam, defeat of, 31, 33–35, 37–38, 67, 70

I

International League of Communists, 23–24
Iran-Contra Scandal, 64

K

KGB, 35
King Jr., Martin Luther, 8, 9
Knights of Malta, 51

L

Lay, Kenneth, 66
Liddy, G. Gordon, 13, 40

M

Mafia, the, 16
megalomaniac, 31
Mein Kampf, 26
military-industrial complex, 34–35
MJ-12, 50–51

N

Nation of Islam (NOI), 8, 10
Nazis, 21, 24, 26–27, 30, 54, 58, 64, 67
"New World Order," 31, 34, 64, 66

Nixon, Richard,
    and JFK assassination, 13, 15–18
    and Watergate, 12–13, 15–18, 50
Nuremberg Trials, 27

O

oil crisis of 1973, 35
Operation Northwoods, 66–67
Organization of Afro-American Unity, 6, 8, 10
Oswald, Lee Harvey, 16, 18, 47

P

Pearl Harbor, attack on, 19, 21–25
Priory of Sion, 57–58, 60

R

Reagan, Ronald, 46, 49–53
Rockefeller, David, 16
Roosevelt, Franklin D., 21–23

S

Skull and Bones Society, 46, 50, 67
Spandau prison, 27, 29, 30

T

Trilateral Commission, 16

U

United Nations (UN), 8, 9, 37
U.S. Department of State, 33, 47

PHOTO CREDITS

Cover *(left)*, pp. 32, 48, 56 Corbis; cover *(right)*, p. 7 Library of Congress; p. 14 Christine Osborne; p. 20 Photri/Topham; p. 28 Keystone Pressedienst/Photos12.com; p.36 Patrick Robert/Corbis; p. 40 Robert Shanna/Corbis; p. 52 USA National Archives/Ronald Reagan Library (NLRR); p. 59 Van Parys/Corbis; p. 65 Brooks Kraft/ Corbis; p. 68 Bob Daemmrich/Corbis.

Designer: Tom Forget

DATE DUE

FEB 6			
MAR 3			
JAN 2 0			

HIGHSMITH 45230